**SERIES 1: AUTHENTIC LIVING AND LEADING**
**BOOK 3**

# AUTHENTIC LEADERSHIP

RECOVERING YOUR DNA
LEADERSHIP-BLUEPRINT

Dr. Brenda Hattingh

Copyright © 2020 by Dr. Brenda Hattingh,

**All rights reserved.**
No part of this book may be used or reproduced and transmitted in any form or by any means, electronic or mechanical, including photocopying, recording, or by any information storage and retrieval system, without signed permission in writing from the copyright owner and publisher.

Cover design by Zander Hattingh
Editing by Copy-Writing: David Barraclough
Graphics by: Gerart Snyman
Email: info@gerart.co.za

ISBN: 9798550853467

**Published by:**
Currency Communications International (Pty Ltd)
Johannesburg, South Africa.

**To order copies of this series:**

order from Amazon books. www.amazon.com/books
See websites:http://www.brendahattingh.com
For more information email: info@powerintelligence.net

# CONTENTS

INTRODUCTION ..................................................................... 5
The Authentic Leadership Community (ALC) ........................... 5
1. What is authentic, quality living? ....................................... 26
2. What is authentic success? ............................................. 27
3. What is leadership? ......................................................... 29
4. What way? – What is the Path? ....................................... 29
5. What is an 'authentic leader'? .......................................... 31
6. Where & when did leadership become necessary? .......... 34
7. The *'Disconnect'* ............................................................ 38
8. What caused the *'Disconnect'*? ..................................... 40
9. What is the 'way' to authentic living and leading? ............ 46
11. How do we find our way back? ........................................ 49
12. Getting reconnected ........................................................ 51
13. The role of DNA in authentic living and leading ............... 55
14. The DNA blueprint and the *Disconnect* ......................... 59
15. Discovering different parts of self ..................................... 61
16. Our higher authentic self, vs shadow ego-self .................. 63
17. The fallacy of current leadership theories, philosophies and 'leadership perspectives' ........................................... 65

| | | |
|---|---|---|
| 19. | Change – from what to what? | 68 |
| 20. | The difference between men and women | 71 |
| 21.. | What authentic living and leading is NOT: | 72 |
| 22. | What authentic living and leading IS | 78 |
| 23. | Summary | 79 |
| Who is the author - dr Brenda Hattingh? | | 82 |
| More books and courses | | 87 |
| References | | 88 |

# INTRODUCTION

## The Authentic Leadership Community (ALC)

**Welcome**

Welcome to the first in a series of books, e-books, and courses to provide you with the latest information, leadership training, and personal development programs on authentic living and leading that includes recovering your DNA success-blueprint while making a difference and being of service to others.

This is a global first in personal and leadership development. The reason is: It contains a whole new mindset with new skills and tools to recover your DNA success-blueprint by using your Power Intelligence – the intelligence of the future.

Irrespective of where and who you are – this is for you!

Prepare yourself for an exciting ride!

## Outside the box

Be prepared for something totally outside the traditional self-help and leadership development paradigm, books, courses, perspectives, philosophies, theories, and teachings.

This new information will challenge your mindset, enlighten your value system, rearrange your thinking, open your mind, and elevate your heart and soul.

Authentic people, especially authentic leaders, are powerful and influential individuals … and very scarce. Life tends to produce them when the world needs them the most.

In a time like – now!

If you are invested in creating a quality future for yourself and that benefits everyone else, then you need to know, the world needs you to stand up and take in your place, now!

## About Authentic Leadership

'Authentic Leadership' was born out of necessity in 2005.

As a lecturer in Industrial and Organisational Psychology at one of the leading universities in South Africa, I also lectured on leadership and leadership development to MBA and M.Com. students at two other universities.

I had to follow the universities' prescribed curriculum.

However, deep down I just knew – we are just doing more of the same. We needed something different and something new. We needed something real and authentic. We needed to think outside the box.

Like the rest of the leadership development industry, I realized that the world was in turmoil. A multibillion-dollar leadership development profession is failing to provide new, quality leaders to meet the challenges of the time.

It became obvious, that we could not keep on doing more of the same just in different packaging if we wanted to create a new quality future and meet current and future demands head-on.

I was embarrassed to give this old, outworn information to the students, but I had to follow the prescribed curriculum.

The time had come for something totally outside the box.

**Getting real**

During this time, my academic background, which included a B.Sc. degree in natural and medical sciences, Honours in Education, Masters in Adult Education, and a Ph.D. in Psychology, kicked in. I came to realise that if we wanted to get real and authentic, our DNA-blueprint (from the background in medical sciences) needed to play a major role, now and in the future.

A whole new personal research project emerged and culminated in the following books seeing the light:

- New Success DNA. What is it and how to develop it[1]
- New Leadership DNA. Developing enlightened leaders[2]
- Power Intelligence. Developing your miracle mind[3]

## Different mindset

My mindset and scope of reference were different from those who were 'leaders' in the field of leadership development. I just knew – the old was over and it was time to move onward and upward. And so, *'Authentic leadership'* was born that included learning how to recover your DNA success-blueprint.

## The academic reaction

Excitement grew as I prepared to present this work with, not only the head of the department but also the dean of the faculty. The hope was to make a contribution, that could put this university in a leadership position where the development of fully functional individuals, teams, companies, and organisations, were concerned. It would be a global first to teach people how to recover their original

DNA success-blueprint and live a quality authentic life while helping others to do the same. We could become *way-showers* where real, authentic leadership is concerned.

## Disappointment and resistance

To my disappointment, this information was met with major resistance from the academics of that time. Initially, I was ignored. When I became more persistent, I was not only was I ostracized, but barriers were deliberately set up to prevent this 'out of the box thinking' from reaching other lecturers, the students, and conferences.

## Deliberately blocked

My papers were blocked from being presented at national conferences and published in local academic journals. Although a few submissions slipped through, the venue was changed on short notice and nobody knew where I was.

The paper to be presented was titled: *DNA – The potential for authentic leaders to emerge.* At a later stage, I, fortunately, got the opportunity to present this topic at *Ted Talks*

To top it all, I was approached by the head of the department who told me to 'back off'.

## Getting over anger and frustration

The natural reaction of anger, resentment, and disappointment made way for a new understanding. The reason was that one of my colleagues and also a friend told me that they had a meeting without me where it was decided to block everything I was doing. The reason was: Five of the Professors and lecturers were planning a book: *Perspectives on leadership.* The book and training courses would be prescribed to all the students and companies and organisations, for the next three years and hopefully be extended to five years.

The authors had created a syndicate and they were in the process of buying holiday homes that would be paid for out of the income of the book/books, courses, and training.

Irrespective of the validity of any new work, they could not allow their plans to be jeopardised by something out of the box.

## Leadership Perspectives

Since then, various books, courses, and training initiatives on *'perspectives on leadership'* have seen light all over the globe. The 'leadership bible' of nearly 600 pages, became available. It contains everybody, who is somebody in the academic and leadership development profession's perspective. Here you find a vast amount of information, opinions, perspectives, theories, and philosophies. There are as many definitions of 'leadership' as there are authors.

All this diverse information just left the students, more confused. I could not stay in this system anymore.

## Fortunate opportunity

Fortunately, the neighbouring university offered me an exciting opportunity. The post included being a liaison between deans of faculties and heads of departments of the university while building bridges with other national and international universities and academic institutions. Not only was a major financial package, title as Professor, and opportunity for international travel included, I would report directly to the Rector of the university, himself.

This post was newly created and opened the opportunity for ground-breaking work of bridgebuilding while creating a culture of academic cooperation and synergy that would benefit everyone.

**Long interview**

During the long and arduous interview, I came to realise many egos were flying around in the room. Irrespective of how qualified and competent I was to fill this post, there was a problem. I was a woman – and I was white.

Something happened during this interview. It was as if my eyes had opened. I saw the ego-battles for survival from all sides play out right in front of me.

This was going nowhere. The sad part was that, after everything; after all the leadership books, courses, training, and coaching, this was the situation and standard of leadership we were presented with.

I got up and walked out… and never returned.

## Getting out of the box

The decision to leave a job with financial security, and research opportunities and privileges of the academic world behind, was initially a difficult decision. The light went up when I realised that if you are going to bring 'out of the box' thinking to the world, then you first needed to get 'out of the box' yourself.

The rest was easy

## Coping with disappointment

Looking back, it was disappointing what I had experienced. At the same time, we must take three things from situations, either positive or negative.

- Find a lesson
- Find the disappointment (sadness/loss)

- Find the funny (find the humour)

It all became clear: The lesson I learnt was – I am not going to change the system. The sadness I found was – I am not going to change the system. The funny I found was – I am not going to change the system.

It was time to move on.

## Why current leadership experts could/will stay behind

Initially, I decided to study the people behind all this information. I asked: Where are they coming from? Does the title of Dr. or Prof. or being an author, qualify you as a real leader? What is authentic leadership?

I found the following: A paradigm shift is taking place. This is a shift in consciousness. It is also a power-shift. Many of our current leaders and leadership experts need to move to the next level.

Some will be able to make this leap – others will stay behind because of:

- Being inflexible and rigid

- Brain blindness/ paradigm blindness
- Over investment in the old paradigm
- Have too much to lose if they shift
- Lack of deeper understanding and intelligence
- Unresolved emotional problems and anxiety
- Shadow ego-self is too strong and won't let go
- Angry and resentful about new developments they didn't create.
- A need to protect themselves and what they have
- Part of the problem
- Self-centred and ego-driven
- Insecurity and fear

Those who will be able to make the shift are

- Flexible
- Prepared to let go of the old and allow new in
- Open-minded and open-hearted
- Know that nothing lasts forever
- Excited to learn something new
- Intelligent and mature
- Emotionally stable and mature

- Wise leaders
- Part of the solution

## Current leadership perspectives and theories

As said, current leadership courses and training initiatives are not producing the quality leaders we now need.

'Leadership' development mostly focuses on 'management' – especially business management. Conference after leadership conference, concede that the world is in turmoil and that we have a 'global leadership crisis'. A multimillion-dollar leadership training industry is still looking for answers …

However, the truth is …

Authentic leaders like Nelson Mandela[4], never attended any leadership training courses or leadership conferences. Madiba was in prison for 27 years. He grew to become an authentic leader, in silence, simplicity, and solitude.

His influence is still relevant today.

## Letting go of the old – embracing the new

So, the question was: Was I going to stay part of the current leadership paradigm – or was it time to 'think-outside-the-box' and go back to the drawing board to find something totally new. Having a look at all the work already published on 'leadership and leadership development', it seems as if all avenues had already been exhausted.

I realised I couldn't stay in a system that kept on repackaging the old in different ways with different names.

If I wanted to 'think outside the box' I first needed to get out of the box and leave it behind. I needed to think for myself and embark on a personal journey of discovery.

I left the academic world, current leadership theories, perspectives and training initiatives, and the people thereof – behind. I also needed to sacrifice my job at the university, the financial freedom it brought, and all resources available in and through the academic world.

Inspired by my four sons, our youth, and also generations to come, I set out on a mission… I asked only one question: What is the Truth about authentic living and leading?

## The Long Walk to Freedom

More than 17 years later I bring you everything I have learnt about authentic living and leading on this long and arduous journey.

It took much longer than I thought it would.

However, now, looking back, I realise that it took time to unlearn a lot of old outworn ideas and to reprogram many things I was taught and took for granted.

I had to detox, detangle, and redefine myself, my new role, a new purpose, and calling, and lay a whole new foundation and start a whole new season of authentic living and leading. Learning from authentic leaders like Nelson Mandela, I came to realise why he called it the *Long Walk to Freedom*.[5]

## Vision and mission of ALC

The vision of the ALC is: *To develop authentic leaders who know the Way, go the Way, and show the Way to authentic self-expression and quality living that benefits all.*

Our mission is to provide cutting-edge personal and leadership assessments, development programs, courses, books, training material, coaching, and mentoring for individuals, teams, and organisations. This includes how to tap into your DNA-blueprint, power, and potential.

**What you will learn at the ALC**

At the Power Intelligence Leadership Academy[6], you will find everything you currently need.

You will find everything you need to know about authentic living and leading. You will also develop a whole new mindset and learn about your unique power and potential encoded as your original DNA success-blueprint.

- **Power Intelligence**

You will learn about the new emerging intelligence, Power Intelligence, the new intelligence you will need to tap into this power and use the potential. You will also become aware of a whole new approach to success, authentic living, and your role as an authentic leader.

The only thing that can stand in your way – is your ego.

- **Some will stay behind**

This means that not everyone will be able to make this shift. Some will rapidly move forward – while others will stay behind.

The ALA will provide all the necessary, assessments, courses, books, coaching and mentoring, training, and support that you will need to lay a whole new foundation for authentic living and leading.

- **Thinking outside the box**

Here you will find 'out of the box thinking' and will be able to identify who will be able to make this quantum leap and who will stay behind. This will help you navigate your new path with your new GPS.

You will find that you too will be able to coach yourself – while walking your *Long Walk to Freedom.* In that way, you will be able to coach and lead others.

- **A new mindset**

With your new mindset, heart-set, skills, and tools, you will not only be able to lead a quality, authentic life as an example for others – you will also be able to take in your place as a powerful, influential, authentic leader and lead just where you are. It's time to get up and take in your place – the world is waiting for you!

Welcome to our new family.

Brenda Hattingh

ooo0ooo

## ABOUT THE SERIES:

## AUTHENTIC LIVING – AUTHENTIC LEADING

In this series we provide you with the latest information, books, courses, coaching, study material, and webinars, covering various different topics of *Authentic living – Authentic leading.*

Each book contains the questions and answers you might ask about these topics. The information is short and to the point. References are included for those who would like to do more research.

The book: Authentic living and leading. *Discovering my DNA success-blueprint*[7] is the flagship book for this series

Each book in the series will cover a topic such as:
- The authentic self. Who am I?
- The authentic self. Coaching yourself to ultimate success
- Authentic leadership. Recovering your DNA leadership-blueprint
- Humanity's leap to authenticity. Where do you stand?
- Authentic living. Miracles and spiritual laws. success
- The quantum leap to authenticity. Will you make it?
- …and others

After this series you will have a whole new mindset and skillset, to take in your place as an authentic leader. You will also be able to live an authentic life of real success.

Find the first 5 books on Amazon's author page: www.amazon.com/author/drbrendahattingh

Follow us on social media:
Twitter:  @DrBrendaInc
Facebook: http://www.facebook.com/DrBrendaInc
LinkedIn: http://www.linkedin.com/Brendahattingh

# OUR NEW JOURNEY OF AUTHENTIC LIVING AND LEADING

*"You cannot bring about change by force –
only by understanding."*
*Einstein*

This is the first in the series of *Authentic Living and Leading* books and courses.

I have summarised the most important information and made it more accessible for everyone – irrespective of who you are, where you are, how old you are, or in what position you are in.[8]

The aim is to provide you with a whole new mindset, cutting edge skills and tools, and a new understanding of quality living and leading. Prepare yourself to be amazed …

So, let's jump right in and try to understand deep and fundamental issues, by asking the right questions and looking for the right answers. This lies in a search for and finding the truth – the fundamental Truth.

This journey is about uncovering the truth of who we are, how we were meant to live, and how to get back to our original state while helping others to do the same. This is also the primary purpose of authentic leaders who take their calling, position, and influence seriously.

So, let's start by asking some fundamental questions:

### 1. **What is authentic, quality living?**

The answer to this question calls for a whole book and course – all on its own. So, if you are serious about walking this path, then enrol for the course: Authentic Living: *Self-coaching for ultimate success*. It also includes the book.[9]

In short, we can summarise this comprehensive topic as:

*'Authentic living is the conscious, mindful ability to master the ego-self by developing your authentic ,encoded as our DNA-blueprint in the process of experiencing life to the full while creating a quality life full of peace, progress, health,*

*wealth, happiness, and service that benefits everyone and nature.'*[10]

For more information on authentic success, see the book: *New Success DNA: What you should know and how to develop it.*[11]


## 2. What is real, authentic success?

Once again, we are confronted with a wide and complicated topic.

However, 'success' is part of life irrespective of what your definition is. It is what most people want to achieve – whatever that may mean to them.

To understanding this topic of 'success' a little more, please see the book *New Success DNA*.[12] Enrol for the short course: *Authentic Living: Understanding ultimate success.*[13]

Here, we can explain the two sides of success: On the one hand, we have the ego-driven success that is motivated by gaining more and more positions and possessions, power positions, and accolades from external onlookers.

Let's look at the real meaning of 'success' a bit closer.

- **The true meaning of success**

On the other hand, we have authentic success, which is inspired by a deeper value system, soul connection, passion, vision, and personal purpose. Fulfillment doesn't lie in the accolades of others – but in achieving your soul calling and personal purpose. You come from internal validation.

The question is: What is the definition of 'real' success.

*'Success is the conscious ability to function authentically'.*


- **Failure**

So, what does failure mean?

*'Failure is the inability to function authentically'.*

Real success is measured by how you function and the quality of person you become n the process and not by what you are accumulating. Wealth doesn't guarantee real success or happiness. It only makes life more comfortable and enjoyable.

## 3. What is leadership?

'Leader' comes from the Latin word – *leido*, which means 'to show the way'. Leadership is the ability to 'show the way'.

The questions are: What way? From what to what? From where to where? Where did it all start? Are we speaking of leadership in general or people in specific positions like a political, business, religious, or community leader?

Let's start with leadership in general and ask: What is the way/Way for all leaders? What one, common path/Path, should we all be following?

## 4. What way? – What is the Path?

Here our first problem concerning 'leadership' emerges. The current dilemmas in the world have arisen because 'leaders' don't agree on a unified definition of 'leadership', a common path, and a clear-cut vision of where the human race should be heading.

Although the United Nations have outlined where we as humanity should be by 2050, each leader and every country still have their own 'perspective on leadership' and how to get to their view of the future. Unity and co-operation towards a common goal is the ultimate solution.

Our challenge is to develop authentic leaders who know the way, go the way, and show the way to authentic self-expression and quality living.

*'Authentic leadership is the conscious ability to show the way to a real-me life and quality living that benefits all including nature'.*

To find out what this means, we need to let go of what we have been programmed with so far, do some unlearning, think outside the proverbial 'box', and open ourselves up to experience something new.

So, let us start by asking some poignant questions.

Let's go back to the beginning, to the roots, and ask: What is the *truth* about a *leader* and *leadership*? What and where are the original roots of leadership? What is real, authentic leadership? Where do *authentic leaders come from*?

## 5. What is an 'authentic leader'?

As previously stated, the word 'leader' comes from the Latin word, *leido*, meaning 'to show the way'.

A leader is a *way-shower, pathfinder,* and *mapmaker.*

They are ones who say: "This is the way/Way". They say: "Follow me – I know the way; I go the way and now I show the way". They show the way by leading by example. They outline a map for those to follow.

The question is:

How does 'authentic' distinguish 'authentic leaders' from other general leaders, or place keepers?

- **Authentic**

'Authentic' comes from the word *author* referring to the original creator, scriptwriter, purpose, foundation, and truth about something or someone.

Authentic refers to what is basic, fundamental, and real.

The flipside is what is false, unreal, untrue, speculation, and delusional.

- **Place keepers**

A place keeper is someone who doesn't 'show the way'. They take up space.

Leaders in specific positions are given special authority to make decisions on behalf of the group and/or masses. Currently, this 'authority' is based on these people having positions and possessions and what we perceive as power.

Positions and possessions do not necessarily teach and qualify you to manage power and authority with integrity – however, we take this for granted. Corruption has become another epidemic of our time.[14]

As we will find out later – the ego is a hard, self-serving taskmaster.

- **Authentic leaders making their mark**

However, *authentic leaders* who made their mark, sometimes come from nowhere and have nothing. Nelson Mandela, Gandhi, and Martin Luther King spent long periods of their life in prison. They rose to positions of power and authority. They didn't care much for positions or possessions. They did however care about achieving their universal purpose and contributing to the greater good. They used power, authority, and their positions, wisely.

They still shine today.

The reason is: Authentic leaders are endowed with special spiritual authority. Because they are universally connected, they have universal authority.[15] They are called, blessed, and 'anointed'. They have the ability to live a selfless life and place themselves in service of all and the greater good.

*Authenticity* and *authority* are flipsides of the same coin.[16]

- **Leadership and calling**

An authentic leader is a person who lives his/her universal calling, purpose, and vision. It is someone who *obtains divine favour* - someone with the *special ability to shine*.

We can identify various authentic leaders of our time that include: Nelson Mandela, Mahatma Gandhi, Martin Luther King, Tolstoy, and others.

More recently, we find people like Bill and Melinda Gates, Barak and Michelle Obama, Oprah, and others. We also find our religious leaders like Buddha, Jesus Christ, and Krishna who made indelible imprints on the fabric of life at different times in history.

- **Authentic leaders are scarce**

Authentic leaders are scarce, have all walked a difficult but unique path, and still shine bright to this day. They emerged when it was their time.

However, we can learn about and even develop these rare qualities that change the world. We can follow in the footsteps of those who have gone before us.[17] We can learn from the best.[18]

We can also shine as an authentic person ... and authentic leader.

So, to help you on this path – let's start at the beginning ...

6. **Where and when did leadership become necessary?**

To find an answer to this question we need to go back to the beginning, to the foundation and roots of humanity, and leadership, and ask: Where did 'leaders' originally come from? Where did 'leadership' all start? Why did it become necessary to have leaders in the first place? Who were the leaders?

We can find our answers in one of Michelangelo's paintings.

- **Learning from a masterpiece**

In the painting below, Michelangelo depicts the beginning and end of all human problems, suffering, illness, poverty, struggle, and stress. On the left side, the Creator is depicted as a young man leisurely relaxing on a planet. Here we find peace, harmony, and a care-free existence without worry, stress, or strain. He is tranquil, without any pressure, rush, lack, sickness, or aging. Restricting forces are absent – including clothing. It is a life of total freedom, wellbeing, connection, love, and compassion.

He is also reaching out to others who are caught up in their circumstances. He is showing the Path back home …

Here we find the first authentic leader in action.

On the other hand, we find humanity depicted as people cramped within a skull, disconnected from the Creator, from the Source. Fear, anguish, pain, despair, and even agony is evident in the cramped space where people are struggling to survive or escape their circumstances.

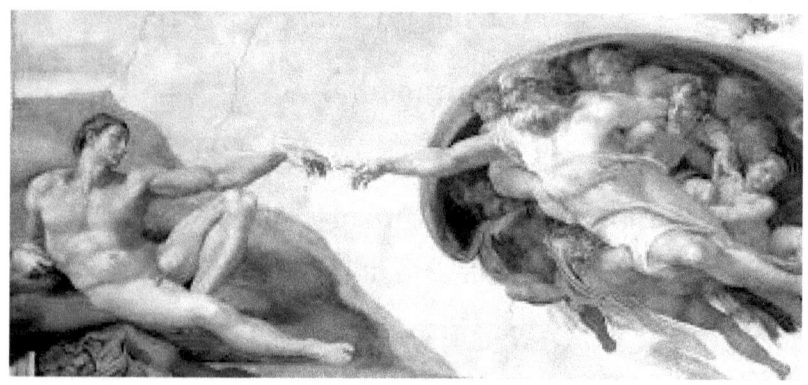

**Sistine Chapel Fresco by Michelangelo. (Pinterest)**

People look lost, sick, aging, and desperate for a solution to their dark, frustrating, meaningless, impoverished, and confusing circumstances

The one positive aspect is a bearded old man (depicting age/wisdom), searching for a solution. He is reaching outside the skull, outside the circumstances, outside the situation people find themselves in. All his efforts are focussed on getting to the root of the real problem. His aim and commitment are to solve the real, source of all dilemmas.

He reaches outside the mind-set and begins to reconnect with Source, the Creator, and the quality of life it brings. He's not struggling with the circumstances and people within the mind-set (skull). He knows something we don't. So do all authentic leaders …

- **Thinking outside the box**

We don't find answers within our current mindsets and thinking strategies Our current, traditional structures, it's systems and the struggles it causes, is represented by the 'skull' or mindset in this painting. The challenge is to first let go and shift your focus outside 'the box/skull', see the solution, put your hand out, and accept the invitation to get reconnected.

- **Our first authentic leaders in action**

Here we find the first, the original authentic leaders in action. Here we find the problem and the solution, exactly in the same place. An authentic leader is someone who knows the way, goes the way and shows the way to a connected life and the fulfilment, and freedom it brings.

The questions are: What caused the disconnection in the first place and how do we fix it? How do we get back to this life of connection and quality living? How do we find our way back?

## 7. The *Disconnect*

Problems started with the *Great Disconnect*. The fabric of life became torn, ripped, and frayed, and allowed darkness in. The pristine circumstances of an authentic, connected life were now traded for the opposite – the *disconnect*. The loss and even absence of health, wealth, happiness, success, love, compassion, peace, harmony, freedom, and progress followed. The world fell into disarray. Humanity got lost. Now we need to find our way back …

## The *Great Disconnect* and the tear in the fabric of life

Now, not only teaching is necessary – we also need healing, cleaning, mending, guidance, and building bridges. Our destination and the solutions to all our challenges are to go back to the origin and source of our issues – and get connected again. This is the path – the way – we need to go.

The route is easy once you know where you are coming from and where you are supposed to go. The reason is: The problem and the solution are exactly in the same place and at the same time. All we needed is understanding.

The questions are: What caused the disconnection in the first place? How do we solve this? How do we find our way? What is the Path?

First, let's find out what caused the *Great Disconnect* in the first place.

## 8. What caused the 'Disconnect'?

Over eons and from many points of view and perspectives, *The Disconnect* has been defined as the 'fall of humanity'. Much has been written, debated, researched – and debated once again. I don't want to reproduce any of this here.

Major religions that include Christianity, Hinduism, the Moslem religion, Shamanism, and others, have discussed this issue from their perspective and provide answers and dogmatic solutions to people who follow their belief systems.

Outside religion, we find science, philosophy, psychology, education, and many other perspectives trying to make sense of and give guidelines for the dilemmas of our time. However, the world is still in confusion.

Below we find a depiction of our current religions. Thank you to the artist.[19]

**Different religions – different paths – one destination**

Once again, the question is: What caused the original *Disconnect*?

The answer covers a vast spectrum of information over many disciplines. Let's make it easy and summarise the main issues from Michelangelo's painting, once again.

Issues that contribute to the Disconnect begin when a person/humanity decide to:

- Disconnect, let go and do their own thing
- Forfeit their innocence, their faith, and serenity

- Disconnect from the universe, the Creator/Source. People, communities, groups or countries let go …
- Let go, go it alone and take control
- Forget, ignore the original aim and Universal Law
- Live within their heads – and make their own laws
- Disconnect from an authentic quality life.
- Let darkness creep in through the cracks in the fabric of life, which causes fear and anxiety
- Fear and anxiety force them to further invest in their mindsets while creating new mindsets with more control and new rules and laws to keep it all in place
- They become delusional while creating their own unreal, twisted view of who they are and what they want/need

- They create an alternative worldview of what health, wealth, happiness, and success are all about
- They do everything to maintain their control
- Anxiety, fear, and anguish grow
- Circumstances deteriorate further
- They fight for the little they think they have
- They struggle with life and try to stay in control
- They find themselves turning on each other
- They find themselves in a downward spiral of self-destruction.
- Anxiety, fear, struggle, fighting, and conflict escalate
- Life conditions deteriorate, with pollution and neglect
- Illnesses and poverty creep in
- Physical, emotional, and mental health issues escalate
- Spiritual poverty is evident

- Religion, science, health services, and education only alleviate the symptoms
- The real underlying cause goes unnoticed and untreated, and it becomes a vicious circle of destruction and devolution
- A Catch-22 situation arises
- People feel trapped, lost, and in despair
- They struggle, fight, and battle to survive
- They become self-centered and are self-serving
- It's a continuous downward spiral –


**Until something happens ... A siren! A wake-up call! A trigger!**

Many wake-up calls are scattered throughout your life. This includes health, financial and/or relationship issues, death, birth or any change. This doesn't always need to be painful – but is usually is. People don't wake up that easy. Do you hear it? Doe you hear the call ? Do you hear the sirens going off or the bells tolling? It is time.

Circumstances will talk you in no uncertain terms.

- You land in difficult circumstances that say - Stop
- You or someone else says: "Stop! There is something better than this. There must be another way …"
- Someone comes and breaks the mold – breaks through the mind-set, looks further than current circumstances, and sees a whole new vision and future
- An authentic leader is born … some-one who reaches out to connect once again
- He/she shows the way by telling/teaching others
- More authentic leaders emerge – those who now know the way, go the way and show the way out of these circumstances.
- These are the individuals, companies, and organisations who take ownership of the circumstances

- Irrespective of where they are and what they have, people decide to turn these circumstances around ...
- People first start within themselves, and then within their immediate family, their friends, and then in their place of work, worship, play, and leisure until they shine globally
- This could be you and me ... It's a matter of choice
- The world is waiting for you to stand up and take in your place! Your time has come.

Now that we know what the problem is – we need to ask: How do we turn this process around? How do we find our way back?

### 9. **What is the 'way' back to authentic living and leading?**

Many eons ago the world looked vastly different from what we experience today. People were connected, centered, and grounded – physically, mentally, emotionally, and spiritually.

People in relationships, marriages, and families all respect themselves, each other, social structures, and the environment. There was honesty, truth, and integrity as joint values. This included peace, harmony, artistic, agricultural, social, economic, and scientific progress, and co-operation.

The most common place of gathering was the temple/s. Here people received teaching from their teachers as priests or priestesses.

The information was downloaded from higher universal dimensions defined as Creator, Source, God/Goddess, or All-that-is. Here *leaders* were primarily teachers. A leader was someone 'to show the way' – one spiritual, universal way, bringing one Truth to everyone.

### 10. One vision, one goal, and one Universal Law

Everyone shared the same goal. The goal was to stay connected, centered, and grounded within the universal Force, stay connected, centered and grounded within the self – and then love others enough to help, assist, teach and guide them to do the same.

- **A common goal**

The result of this common goal was a people and a world in peace and harmony with happiness and fulfilment, which benefitted everyone.

This was the most important Universal Law to live by. It still is today …

- **A common law**

This common law and vision were taught to children from a young age. They learnt to understand their personal and collective purpose and the meaning of life and life-purpose, from a young age.

Adults went about their daily chores while everyone was mindful, conscious, and deeply aware of the opportunity to be living in a physical body on a planet called Mother Earth.

The goal was to experience this physical life on Earth, with the challenges and opportunities, to the full. The good and the bad.

- **Fully functional**

Everyone was fully functional, in a state of peace, love, compassion, power, passion, and flourished as a human race. This was the ultimate state of human-existence – 'as heaven on Earth' – Utopia, Nirvana.

What is more important is that this 'end goal' as a destination, is already encoded as a primary DNA blueprint in every cell of every person.

This is how we were created to be and to live our lives. Now we are returning to our original blueprint state.

## 11. How do we find our way back?

The Path back is easy. It's found in our DNA-blueprint.

Below you see what this path should look like … See course three in this series of authentic living and leading, entitled: *DNA – Climbing the new ladder of success.*

Have a closer look at Michelangelo's painting once again and identify different steps that need to be taken, to return to our original position.

Here are some steps we need to take into consideration.

**Finding your way back**

**Steps to finding your way back**

- Become aware of current personal and global circumstances
- Remind yourself that this is only symptomatic
- Remember, the map can be found as your DNA-blueprint
- Remember – the real problem is the Disconnect
- Don't struggle with the symptoms and disconnection

- Alleviate symptoms and circumstances where you can
- Stop – don't struggle with what you don't want by investing any emotional energy in these negative circumstances
- First, turn the circumstances around within yourself – just where you are
- Break free from restricting mindsets and outworn perspectives
- Go within – Let go of struggling with that without
- Develop a whole new vision – focus on what you do want
- Focus on getting reconnected again
- Follow the steps outlined in the courses
- The rest will unfold – step for step.

Our questions are: How do I get reconnected? How do I recover my DNA success-blueprint? What must I know and do?

## 12. Getting reconnected

We first need to find out where this 'connection is'. Is there a switch, lever, switchboard, or control panel, that we can enable?

The answer to all our problems would, of course, be easy if we could just flip a switch. Unfortunately, it's a bit more complicated than that, as we have a whole switchboard that needs to be reactivated.

Most people who are invested in training, HR-development, coaching and mentoring, focus on neurodevelopment, mind-power, thinking skills, and/or neurophysiology. However, we need to go deeper and further to get to the roots – to the source/Source of connection and getting connected. We have to reach down right to our DNA-blueprint.

The beginnings of the body of any human being start with DNA. A string of RNA of the mother and RNA of the father join, connect, unite, and trigger a whole new life-force, and process of life, into being.

However, we are more than a body – we are also connected to the universal grid, Source, Universal Soul, Spirit, Creator, or God. So, we also have a spiritual connection to the universal grid and a personal connection to our original soul.[20]

Here DNA also plays a role.

- **A bit of background to understand this better**

We function as a unified whole that includes body, mind, soul, and spirit. When we became disconnected on a universal level (fall from grace), our original life-force becomes depleted. We run on half-measures, near to empty. We have to pressurise, stress, strain, and struggle to make things work. Our energy resources, our life force, becomes depleted and the rest begins to slowly disintegrate.

Very seldom are soul and spiritual connections included in education and training - especially leadership training. Most courses focus on skills, tools, and brainpower. Soul and spiritual connections are a separate compartment/department and are left to religion to cover.

However, science has found that DNA is at its peak functioning at a certain frequency, wavelength, or resonance. Lower frequencies and wavelengths can impair genetic functioning and can even disconnect the genetic power and potential further.

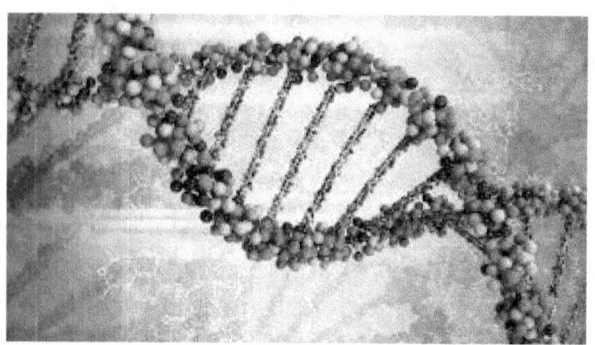

**DNA - our blueprint for authentic living and leading**

This not only fragments the fabric of life still further – it can lead personal and leadership education, training, and development initiatives down many stray and/or strange paths.

- **Optimizing your DNA success-blueprint**

Scientists have identified this universal frequency like 528 Hz. It's a universal frequency that runs in and through everything and everyone and binds everything and everyone into a unified, harmonious, fully functional whole. We can restore this resonance as it is found in human beings as happiness, love, and compassion.

People can be taught to elevate themselves and evolve to this level of consciousness and awareness, once again. For this we need a special, fourth dimension intelligence, as Power Intelligence, to activate this frequency again. See Book 2 and course two: Power Intelligence: What is it and why you need it now.

## 13. The role of DNA in authentic living and leading

Everything everyone needed to know, understand, and to create this world, was originally encoded as a DNA-blueprint in every cell of every single human being. Everything was active and fully functional. The only purpose was to find out where you can be of service and how to enjoy life to the full.

Life was simplistic[21] and uncomplicated …

- **DNA – a barcode**

The reason is: This DNA-code, called a DNA-barcode, can open doors, elevate thinking, trigger new, exciting events, attract new people, and initiate co-operation, love, compassion, and progress.

The people or groups who are on the same wavelength can share the same DNA blueprint of health, wealth, happiness, and prosperity and function as one unified whole. This is just like a school of fish that functions as a unified, synergised whole, although it consists of hundreds, even thousands of individual small fish. [22] This is called Epigenetics.[23]

In ages gone by, overseers ensured that the younger ones lived their soul-purpose and became and remained fully functional. They were taught to develop and express their own unique abilities and gifts for the benefit of everyone. They were taught to be of a unique service to all.

Everyone joined in each other's progress and accomplishments.

Here 'success' was defined by the way you become fully functional, fulfil your soul purpose and calling, and enjoy life to the full. It refers to the activation of your special unique Success DNA. [24] Positions and possessions had no meaning, except to make life comfortable and enjoyable.

- **DNA and leadership**

Authentic leadership is not determined by your power position and physical possessions – it is determined by the fact that you are highly conscious, mindful and aware, connected, centered and grounded, and understand the ultimate goal of Real-me, authentic self-expression, and quality living. You have walked the path. Now you can place yourself in service to show others 'the way'.

*An authentic leader is someone who knows the way, goes the way, and shows the way to authentic self-expression and quality living and authentic leading that benefits all.*

Each authentic leader has a general goal and a specific goal, calling, or purpose. The general goal is to live an authentic life and to set an example. The specific goal is to show the way and lead from just where you are.

You can be a CEO of a large Fortune 500 company, in government, delivering professional services, be a teacher, parents, friend, spouse, or student. The position is not the issue here ... the quality of your influence is. Lead from just where you are ... you were placed there for a reason.

Remember – Earth is round with no beginning and end. You are always on the center stage – just where you are!

Question: How do I become real, authentic, and fully functional?

- **Taking responsibility**

You identify and discern between your connected and disconnected parts of self.

You take responsibility for the quality of person you are and are becoming. You decide which part of self you would like to express. Then you learn how – and you practice ... every moment – every day.[25]

You take back your power, heal the parts that are broken, collect and re-integrate the fragmented parts, and identify a whole new vision. You can then become the real you, the authentic you, the best part of the self.

You begin to live the best version of yourself, the best self you can be living, and the best life you can have. You can have it all …

The question is: How?

## 14. The DNA blueprint and the *Disconnect*

At a deep, fundamental level – we find our universal blueprint and the disconnection, evident in our DNA. The problem and solution are exactly in the same place at the same time. When scientists identified these disconnected DNA parts in the human genome, they didn't know what the purpose thereof was.

They defined it as 'junk DNA' or 'junk genes'… and ignored further investigation.

This was until the Human Genome Project revealed the power and potential encoded in 'junk genes'.

Up and till now, we took for granted that our DNA-sequence was a given, something you were born with, and that was cast in stone – something we were born with and have to live with. However, today, we understand that if we become more aware and raise our consciousness, we can mindfully reconnect our DNA. We can tap into this power and potential while putting it to good use for the benefit of all – if we know-how.

This goes beyond current tertiary educational systems as we move to a quaternary (fourth) level, where we find quantum thinking. It is from this level where we find our authentic leaders now emerging.[26]

As previously stated, DNA functions at an optimum level at a specific vibe, resonance, frequency, or wavelength. Scientists have identified this universal frequency as 528 Hz. We can restore this resonance as it is found in human beings, as happiness, love, and compassion.

People can be taught to elevate themselves and evolve to this level of consciousness and awareness, once again.

This is where we will spend our next season of research, development, and training – especially leadership training.[27]

It's very easy. The reason is that this is our natural state. We are only returning to what was our original birth-right encoded as a DNA-blueprint, our original self, higher self, authentic self, the real self, our best self, or the brightest self.

Unfortunately, with the Disconnect – we now have two, even many fragmented parts of self. If so – which me – which part of self – can have it all?

## 15. Discovering different parts of self

As said, we have two parts of self. On the one side we have a connected, centered, grounded, and enlightened part of self.

On the other hand, we have a disconnected, shadow, ego-self.

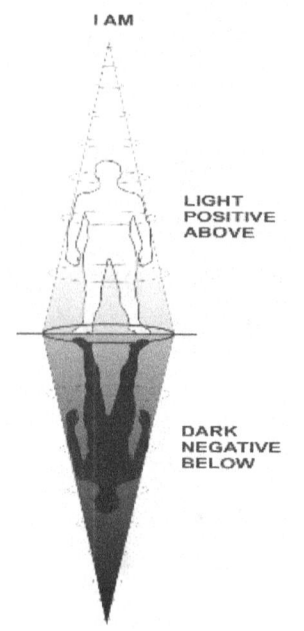

The real, authentic, best, real-me self, strives to become more and more connected, centered, and grounded – while aiming to raise the bar – the resonance and become more of service.

It focuses on living an authentic, quality life that benefits everyone and nature. To achieve this, we need to become more conscious, aware, and mindful.

On the other side, the shadow ego-self is disconnected, living different shades of grey, while struggling mindlessly to survive in a boxed-in worldview that seems dark, depressing, negative, and meaningless.

It is a constant process of devolution as one negative thought, act, word, or choice, leads to another.

In the end, self-destruction is inevitable.

So, what happens when these two sides of self, clash?

## 16. Our higher authentic self, versus shadow ego-self.

Each side comes from a different value-system and different point of view. These are opposing forces and there is a constant battle going on as these two value-systems clashes. Just think, all this is going on within the same person!

There is also a constant inner battle, an inner noise, going on between the two parts of self. These unseen inner conflicts and battles spill over into life. We then see this as 'problems'.

All problems and conflicts are just symptomatic of the dynamics going on with each individual, within the situation.

| VALUE-CENTRED | EGO-CENTRED |
|---|---|
| Self-aware | Self-conscious |
| Self-worth | Self-centered |
| Self-esteem | Self-importance |
| Self-care | Self-serving |
| Self-confidence | Self-delusion |
| Self-respect | Self-indulgence |
| Self-mastery | Self-destructive |

## The authentic self vs the shadow ego-self

Above your find a summary of the different connections and different value-systems

The solutions to solving our outer battles are easy. First, solve your inner battles, get real, get connected, and bring your best self to the table.

Once you become aware of this, you can stop the conflict, take action, and turn the process around while directing the energy to your best advantage and a win-win situation for all.

**A constant battle between the different parts of self**

Teams, families, groups, companies, and/or organisations function in the same way – just at a larger scale.

This is what causes conflict, resistance, discord, and hinders progress, growth, and development, within business, governments, organisations, and humanity as a whole.

All we need to do is to learn how to turn the process around!

The solution is easy if you become aware of the true underlying causes of our current personal and collective challenges, ask for the truth, and learn how to turn the process around.

The question is: If this path is so easy and uncomplicated, then why all the diverse leadership definitions, leadership theories, perspectives, conferences, gatherings, training schools, and all their opinions?

## 17. The fallacy of current leadership theories, philosophies and perspectives

Another question: Why don't all the theories and perspectives on leadership 'show the way'? The answer is easy: because these theories and perspectives only consider part of the picture. It is then enlarged to make us think this is the whole picture. It is only a perspective and theory – not necessarily the whole truth.

It is like looking at an elephant through a straw and defining what it is: Some say it looks like a big leaf or ear; others see a whip that could be a tail; others see two teeth that that look like a front-end loader; others see a hose that looks like a trunk or a mountain on stilts that could be a body. All have a part of the picture. However – none of the parts represent the whole.

**The whole elephant is more than the separate parts.**

We first need to stop, stand back, and have a new look at what we are trying to achieve. Then we will be able to identify the big picture – and it will make more sense. We must change our point of view …

Authentic living and leading must include our DNA success-blueprint and recovering our power and potential.

We need a whole new vision of the future, of 'leadership' and a radical change in our current mindset if we want to secure a quality future.

We even need a whole new intelligence as Power Intelligence (PI) – The intelligence of the future. As human beings, we need to maintain the balance between humanity and the machine.

## 18. Artificial Intelligence (AI) and Power Intelligence (PI)

As Artificial Intelligence (AI) grows, takes over many functions, and makes more and more decisions on our behalf, we need to develop our human potential and keep raising our consciousness at the same pace. We need to stay ahead.

As described, this power and potential are encoded as a DNA blueprint. We need a new kind of intelligence, consciousness, and awareness to recover and release this power and potential.

We need *Power Intelligence.*

*Power Intelligence is the conscious ability to tap into, release, harness, and utilize, our infinite power and potential encoded as a DNA blueprint and put it to positive use to the benefit of all.*

Authentic leaders are highly conscious of how they use their personal and positional power. Authentic leadership and Power Intelligence go hand in hand. It's time for a change. It's time for a power-shift and a quantum leap ...

## 19. Change – from what to what?

The challenge is to put everything we have learned about 'leaders' and 'leadership' aside (don't discard it because it has a place), open our minds, think outside the box, go back to the drawing board, and ask new questions.

As we open our minds and hearts and see the bigger picture, a whole new world will become clearer. Not alone is a whole new part, a fourth part of the brain now coming into action. We are also developing a whole new intelligence.

Power Intelligence is the intelligence of the future.

We are moving to the fourth level of education and training as tertiary education takes a back seat and quaternary education and quantum thinking emerge.

We will be focussing on this shift and new development in book 2 of series 1, entitled: Power Intelligence: What is it and how to develop it.

In the meantime, I include the picture/diagram below so you can begin to wrap your mind around it.

You will need this information on your journey of becoming an authentic person, especially an authentic leader.

Once we've grown in our awareness and raised our consciousness, the rest will follow, fall into place and begin to make sense.

This will boost our progress as we identify a new vision with substance, meaning, and purpose that benefits all.

The reason is: The whole is greater than the individual parts. The big picture brings deeper meaning and fundamental understanding, purpose, and knowing.

Not many people reach this higher level.... Most will stay behind and become followers.

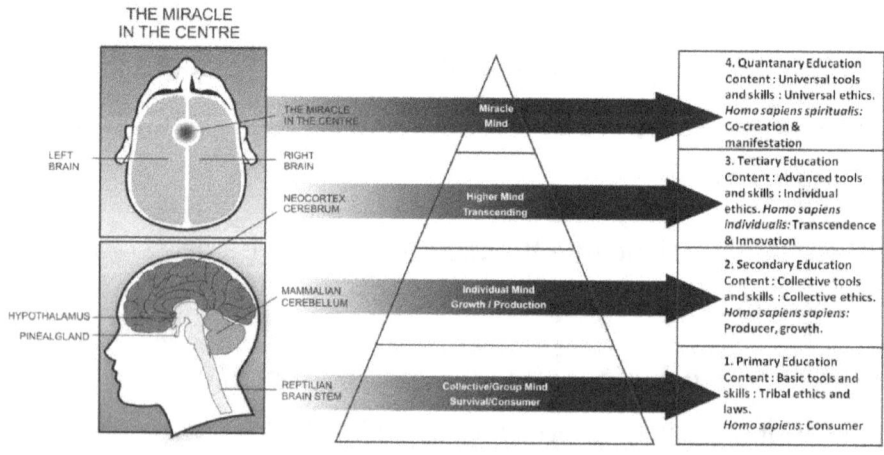

**Quaternary education and quantum thinking**

For those of us who accept this challenge, start at the beginning, and take it step-by-step from there. Remember it takes time – its life!

A leader like Nelson Mandela called this the 'Long Walk to Freedom'.

This too is our challenge.

## 20. The difference between men and women

Men and women differ not only because they have different brains, but they also differ right down to a DNA level. The gender chromosome for women contains the XX chromosome, while men have an XY chromosome.

This initially small difference has major implications for the whole life of an individual.

The moment the birth of a 'boy' or a 'girl' is announced, subconscious social programming already takes place in respect of how this baby should be raised.

In the past, boys have always been favoured for leadership roles.

In the past, girls were programmed to take in more subservient roles and positions. This doesn't necessarily apply anymore.

There are however still countries that suppress their women.

The world is changing. A *Power Shift* is taking place.

Women, real authentic women, make this shift easier than men. The reason is that most women don't build their whole lives on ego-investments as most men do.

- **Ego-driven**

Unfortunately, today we still have arrogant, ego-driven men in immensely powerful leadership positions. They daily reveal their self-serving motives in their homes, the workplace, in churches, and even in business and politics.

But now this is changing …

This powershift is part of the 'female' nature as it requires compassion and caring. The call is for a balanced development of masculine and feminine traits – an androgenic personality.

- **Leadership development for girls**

Leadership development where girls and women are concerned is one of our greatest challenges. The reason is: Here we will find hidden power and potential that will and can take us further than we have ever imagined. By investing leadership development in girls, we will fast forward the power-shift, to the benefit of everyone.

The challenge is to develop authentic living and leading for boys and girls as part of a balanced education, from a young age.

This kind of quality, holistic, integrated education, benefits everyone. It takes a mature, connected, centred, grounded, and balanced persona to overcome his/her egos, and accept this.

## 21. What authentic living and leading is NOT?

In the beginning, we asked a few poignant questions, like:

- What is authentic living and leading?
- What is authentic success?
- What role does DNA play in this process?
- What is Power Intelligence?
- What is the underlying problem of current leadership and training initiatives?

I've given some answers as a summary of more than 10 years of academic, medical, scientific, and universal research to find answers to fundamental and universal questions. If you are interested in this background, please see the following books:

- New success DNA: What is it and how to develop it
- Power Intelligence: Developing the miracle mind
- New Leadership DNA: Developing enlightened leaders.

These books are available on <u>Amazon's Brenda Hattingh Page</u>

As with any other new time, place, and challenge, we also find new 'buzz words' emerging.

Many people jump on the bandwagon and give their opinions, perspectives, ideas, and assumptions to be 'first in line with something new'. And so it happens that we find diverse ideas, and perspectives on authenticity, the real self, the authentic self, the best self, success, and now authentic leadership emerging and finding their way onto the platforms of life.

The question is: How does this series in authentic living and leading differ from the current perspectives emerging?

Let's first take a look at what authentic living and leading – *is not.*

**Authentic living and leading are NOT:**

- Not – Just another perspective, theory, assumption, and idea we need to deal with and sift through among all the other assumptions, ideas, and philosophies cluttering our lecture rooms, bookstores, conference halls, and training corridors
- Not – another 'lofty idea', 'flavour of the week' or 'buzz-word of the year' concept
- Not – a here today and gone tomorrow assumption
- Not – something you/we just philosophy about in arm-chair discussions, lecture rooms, or over coffee
- Not – simply good sounding concepts, but without substance, grounding, meaning, and purpose

- Not – old and camouflaged material, just in a new packaging
- Not - in competition with anything else or anyone on the current market
- Not – like everything else you've heard of before
- Not – something that has just suddenly arrived as if 'out of the blue'. It's always been there. We are the ones who became disconnected, lost the plot, lost our way, and created a life of delusion
- Not – a power-game that is driven by the shadow ego-self
- Not – for the faint-hearted. And we can go on ….
-

The question is: Then what is authentic living and leading?

## 22. Authentic living and leading:

- Is – the real, authentic original way of life as it is supposed to be. It is the truth…
- Is – uncomplicated, straight forward, and visible to the honest eye, open heart, and clear mind
- Is – the mental, emotional, physical, and spiritual journey we have been born for on this physical planet we call Mother Earth
- Is – connected, centred, rooted, and grounded in the most fundamental grounding of universal law, truth, and existential essence of humanity
- Is – the fundamental essence of real success and happiness
- Is – who we have always meant to be
- Is – rooted in truth, honesty, and integrity

- Is – the result of the connection to the deepest roots of our personal and universal power, wisdom, and compassion … for our self, and others
- Is – living the authentic, real, or best part of self and creating a quality life that benefits all
- Is – the result of following the map for a successful personal and collective journey, encoded as a DNA blueprint in every cell of our body
- Is – the journey of life in search of the truth – a spiritual journey
- Is – the result of our awakening and growing awareness
- Is – the path of personal and collective freedom. 'Truth sets you free'
- Is – the path Nelson Mandela called *'The long walk to freedom'*
- Is – encoded as a DNA blueprint of truth, power, potential, and wisdom. We just need to discover, connect to, release, and use these gifts
- Is – the challenge everyone needs to accept and contend with
- Is – The symbol of the next stage of human development and evolution
- Is – teachable. We can teach people to think, live and lead authentic lives and become authentic leaders[28]
- Is – our natural state
- Is – always within our reach, attainable and accessible
- Is – for everyone. However, not all will reach this stage and level of consciousness and awareness.

They can and will remain imprisoned in darkness, driven by fear, and the shadow ego-self

- Is – always there and has always been there. It is us, who got disconnected and lost our way.
- Is – the key to meaning, purpose, and personal and collective calling
- Is – more than an idea or philosophy… it is a science. As a science, it is '*a systematically organized body of knowledge on this particular subject*'
- Is – Truth and is measurable, duplicate-able, and repeatable This means we will keep getting to the same answer to our questions – about the essence and the roots of our search into authentic living and leading, irrespective of who we are, where we are, and what route we take. Truth is truth.
- Is – a fact that unites us all. The only choice you have is to accept this path or not
- Is – the way to health, wealth and happiness and real success
- Is – a call to you to stand up and take your rightful place
- Is – the challenge for you to make a difference
- Is – your responsibility to lead others and say: 'I know the Way, I go the Way and show that Way'
- Is – the ability to love and be loved and live with compassion
- Is – for the fearless, the lion-hearted. It's called 'gutsy living'
- Is – here to stay. This is the beginning of our next season

Take the list above and mark what you already know and what you still need to learn.

Focus on developing these issues

## 23. Summary

To summarise your new understanding after reading this book and doing the course, ask yourself the following questions:

- What is authentic living?
- What is authentic leading?
- What role does DNA play in authentic living and leading?
- What caused the disconnect?
- What is the real role of authentic leaders in general?
- What is the role of authentic leaders in their circumstances?
- Why are all the leadership theories, perspectives, and a multibillion-dollar global leadership business, not producing authentic leaders that the world needs now?
- What part would you like to play?
- Are you aware of your ego and that it can be delusional and destructive?
- Can you identify your ego-self and where it is coming from?
- Can you coach your ego into a more functional and healthier position?

- How are you currently developing your authentic self?
- What can you do to boost your development and transformation into an authentic leader and make the difference the world is waiting for?
- What is authentic living – NOT?
- Now that you have gone through these processes – what do you say is authentic living and leading?

## 24. What next?

This is only the beginning of this journey. It's only the tip of the iceberg. There is still a long way to go

Follow series 1 with all the books and courses on authentic living and leading:

- Book 1: The authentic self. Who am I?
- Book 2. Coaching your self to ultimate success
- Book 3: Authentic Leadership: Recovering your DNA leadership-blueprint
- Book 4: Power Intelligence – The intelligence of the future
- Book 5: DNA – Climbing the new ladder of success.
- Book 6: The quantum leap to authenticity. Will you make it?

More books and courses in this series will be released later in 2021.

For books see: Amazon's Brenda Hattingh Page

Join our mailing list available <u>here and get book one free</u>

Get your free *Daily Power Tools for power People* delivered to your inbox <u>here.</u>

For courses see the <u>Power Intelligence Leadership Academy here</u>

ooo0ooo

## WHO IS THE AUTHOR - DR BRENDA HATTINGH?

Dr. Brenda Hattingh is an international inspirational speaker, leadership coach and mentor, and business, corporate, and leadership consultant. Brenda invests her time in using personal and organisational power and success potential encoded as our unique DNA blueprint. This is a global first in personal and organisational training and development.

Brenda is committed to the development of a new level of consciousness with an awareness of the value of authentic living and leading. She focuses on assisting people, teams, companies, and organisations – who are willing to bring their *best selves* to the table.

As an author, Brenda brings to the table cutting edge information, books, and training courses that include topics *like Power Intelligence – the intelligence of the future, New Success DNA*, and *New Leadership DNA*. She is Director of the *Power Intelligence Academy* and *The Academy for Authentic Leaders*. Brenda is also the *CEO of the Centre for Power Intelligence*

As an innovator, Brenda is committed to the development of a new generation of successful, innovative, inspired, thinkers, and leaders. She speaks at events and conferences, presents workshops nationally and internationally, lectures at various universities, and has published various books.

Her work is featured on TEDx Talks as Brenda introduces the next season of personal development and leadership training that includes tapping into your DNA-blueprint. Brenda is also the recipient of various awards including the
*Professional Businesswoman of the Year Award.*

**OoooOooo**

**ENROLL FOR A PERSONAL 5-WEEK COURSE.**

**LEARNING TO COACH YOURSELF TO ULTIMATE SUCCESS**

This will be one of the best investments you have ever made.

**Background**

Times have changed and we need to think on our feet. You can only be super successful and flourish if you know how to coach yourself and manage your inner dialogue. Very few people, especially leaders, know how to do this.

At the moment, we are also experiencing a genetic migration. Humanity is going through a transformation, right down to a DNA level. This means we also need to learn how to activate our DNA success-blueprint. The information on how to do this is now available.

Contact us if you would first like to book a free session

**What will you learn?**

In this beginner course of *Learning to Coach Yourself*, that runs over five weeks, you will learn:

- Who your real-me is and what your personal purpose is
- How to tap into and activate your DNA success-blueprint
- How to master your inner dynamics and create affluence
- How to create the next level of success and happiness
- How to overcome inner blockages and pitfalls
- To understand the psychology of money and affluence
- To understand the science and psychology of real success
- How to become an authentic leader and influencer
- How to create health, wealth, and happiness that benefits everyone
- And much more…

**What will you receive:**

- E-book 1. Coaching yourself to ultimate success. Who coaches who?
- E-book 2: Authentic living and leading. What is it and how to develop it
- Your personal workbook for your notes
- Five one-on-one personal coaching sessions via Skype, Zoom, or WhatsApp with Dr. Brenda Hattingh.
- Three DNA-healing sessions
- A plan of action
- /map for the next season of your life.


**Who should invest in this course?**

Everyone who wants to move forward and create their best life. This includes people like you and me, leaders, teachers, parents, business-people, couples …

Books available on Amazon's Brenda Hattingh Page

**How to book your *Course. Learning to coach yourself?***

Send an email to: info@powerintelligence.net. We will send all the necessary information to your inbox.

See our website: http://www.brendahattingh.com

**This course is also Available for team building, and leadership development in companies and organisations.**

oooOooo

## BOOK DR BRENDA HATTINGH AS SPEAKER

To book Dr. Brenda Hattingh as an exciting, entertaining, and inspirational speaker for your next event, or conference and training session, contact us by sending an email to:

Email: info@powerintelligence.net

See website: http://www.brendahattingh.com

oooOooo

## BOOK DR BRENDA FOR LEADERSHIP TRAINING

Email us: info@powerintelligence.net

OoooOooo

## MORE BOOKS AND COURSES

For books see:  Amazon's Brenda Hattingh Page

Or contact us: info@powerintelligence.net

Books Avaible on  Amazon's Brenda Hattingh Page

# REFERENCES

[1] Hattingh, Brenda (2012.a.). *New Success DNA. What is it and how to develop it.* Currency Communications: Johannesburg.

[2] Hattingh, Brenda. (2012. c) *New Leadership DNA. Developing enlightened leaders.* Currency Communications. Pty.Ltd.: Johannesburg.

[3] Hattingh, Brenda. (2012.b) *Power Intelligence. Developing your miracle mind.* Currency Communications. Pty. Ltd.: Johannesburg.

[4] Hattingh, Brenda. (2020). *Life Lessons from Nelson Mandela about lockdown.* Currency Communications: Johannesburg.

[5] Hattingh, Brenda (2020). *Life Lessons from Nelson Mandela about lockdown.* Currency Communications Pty.Ltd.: Johannesburg

[6] Power Intelligence Leadership Academy website: https://power-intelligence-leadership-academy.teachable.com

[7] Hattingh, Brenda. (2020) *The authentic self. Discovering my DNA success-blueprint.* Currency Communications. Johannesburg

[8] You will find all the research on the list of books in the references below.

[9] Hattingh, B.E. (2020). *Authentic Living. Coaching yourself to ultimate success.* Currency Communications Pty Ltd: Johannesburg.

[10] Hattingh, B.E. (2012a). *New Success DNA. What you should know and how to activate it.* Currency Communications Pty Ltd: Johannesburg.

[11] Hattingh, Brenda (2012.a.). *New Success DNA. What is it and how to develop it.* Currency Communications: Johannesburg.

[12] Hattingh, B.E. (2012a). *New Success DNA. What you should know and how to activate it.* Currency Communications Pty Ltd: Johannesburg.

[13] See Short course: *Authentic Living: Understanding ultimate success.* More details on the website.

[14] Hattingh, Brenda. (2020) Corruption. *Seven steps to curing the epidemic of our time.* Currency Communications.: Johannesburg.

[15] See the book in the Series: Authentic Living and Leading:

Hattingh, B.E. (2019) *Authentic leaders and authority.* Currency Communications Pty Ltd: Johannesburg. Available June 2020.

[16] The word 'authority' comes from the Latin '*auctor*' meaning, 'author', which refers to someone who can write - write a law, script, or set guidelines. In short, it refers to a 'pathfinder' or 'mapmaker'. An authentic leader is a person as someone *who obtains divine favour* - someone with the special *ability to shine*.

[17] See: Hattingh, B.E. (2014) *Seven steps to securing the Madiba Magic in life and leadership.* Currency Communications Pty Ltd: Johannesburg.

[18] See ALA course: *Authentic Leadership: Learning to think, live, and lead like Nelson Mandela.*

[19] Artist unknown.

[20] For more information, see the series: *Authentic Living: Coaching yourself to ultimate success:*

Hattingh, B.E. (2020) *Authentic living: Going back to your roots.* Currency Communications Pty Lt: Johannesburg.

[21] See the book in the series: *Authentic Leaders in action:*

Hattingh, B.E. (2020). *Authentic leadership and Triple-S for success. Solitude, silence, and simplicity.* Currency Communications Pty Ltd: Johannesburg. Available; Aug 2020

[22] See the series of Authentic Living and Leading on:

Hattingh, B.E. (2019). *Authentic leadership and epigenetics. A new path to building fully functional, teams, groups, companies, and organisations.*Currency Communications Pty Ltd: Johannesburg.

[23] Epigenetics: Our DNA is influenced by the environment, but we too can make a genetic imprint on and change our environment.

See: Book 3 with course three, entitled: *DNA: Climbing the new ladder of success.* Available: Feb 2021.

[24] Hattingh, B.E. (2012a). *New Success DNA. What you should know and how to activate it.* Currency Communications Pty Ltd: Johannesburg.

[25] The necessary courses are available at the Authentic Leadership Academy. https://power-intelligence-leadership-academy.teachable.com

[26] The book in this series: *Authentic Leaders in action:*

Hattingh, B.E. (2020) *Authentic living and leading: Quantum thinking and quaternary education.* Currency Communications. Johannesburg.

[27] Hattingh, B.E. (2012b) *New Leadership DNA. Developing enlightened leaders*. Currency Communications Pty Ltd: Johannesburg.
[28] See: https://power-intelligence-leadership-academy.teachable.com

ooo0ooo

www.ingramcontent.com/pod-product-compliance
Lightning Source LLC
Chambersburg PA
CBHW070810220526
45466CB00002B/624